The Pilgrim's Progress

Leader's Guide

DRC Films, LLC
ReelChristian.com

Special thanks to our small group Bible Study where I met my wife Aubrey: Thank you Aubrey, Christy, Jess, Katie, Kris, Mindy, Shelah, Tiffany, Trisha, and Tracie.

For more information:

DRC Films, LLC
PO Box 3825
McAllen, TX 78502

Guide written by Steve Gardner. Contact: steveandmariagardner.com

Contents

What the Leader Needs to Know

This small group study employs the inspirational power of the visual story and enables participants to explore and apply its practical truths.

Each of the six sessions is based on a 15-20 minute segment of the Pilgrim's Progress DVD.

Suggested Format and Time Allotment

These times are reasonable allocations for a 1:15 total meeting time. Adjust as necessary for your format and available time.

1. Present the Introduction (a brief review/preview in the Leader's Guide. NOTE: This may be presented on the video at the beginning of each segment). 5 minutes

2. Watch the video segment. Do not attempt to follow the Video Notes while watching the video. 20 minutes

3. Lead the group through the Video Notes. 15 minutes

4. Interact with the group (guided discovery) to help them determine the fill-ins.

5. All underlined words in the Leader's Guide are fill-ins (___) in the Participant Guide.

- Bold words in the accompanying verse (in both Leader's and Participant Guide) correspond to the fill-ins.

- Consider allowing the participants to alternate reading Video Note entries. A good procedure is to have someone read the entry (with blanks) followed by the accompanying verse(s). In most cases, the fill-in will then be obvious.

- Any of the Video Notes statements can lead to meaningful discussion opportunities. Be open to questions or comments from the group during this time.

6. Lead the group discussion with two kinds of questions. 25 minutes

   - Questions from participants

   - Questions printed in the Guide

   - The Leader's Guide contains some suggested answers [in brackets] for questions that are less subjective. These answers do not appear in the Participant Guide.

   - If the group has more than five people, consider subdividing for the Discussion Questions. This allows everyone to participate in a more meaningful way.

7. Give the group three minutes to write the Application: What will you start doing, stop doing or do differently this week in light of what you have seen or heard in this session? 5 minutes

8. Allow volunteers to share something from their Application. 3 minutes

9. Close with prayer. 2 minutes

Session 1: The Journey Begins

"The prudent see danger and take refuge [flee from it], but the simple keep going and suffer for it."
Proverbs 22:7

Introduction

Pilgrim's Progress was written in 1675 by John Bunyan, a poor tradesman from Bedford, England, who was jailed for preaching the Word of God. He wrote it while in prison.

The entire story is a dream, so when you see scenes that seem surreal, they are! In these scenes we catch glimpses of Satan's favorite deceptions, the ones he has used successfully throughout the ages in his effort to derail us.

The story begins with a dramatic dilemma—a husband and wife with opposing worldviews. And these worldviews are like oil and water; they cannot be blended into something acceptable to both. Right and wrong, truth and error, light and darkness—all of these really do exist. And they matter. Not all roads lead to heaven, particularly the most heavily traveled.

Although it would be arrogant to say we understand everything God is doing and by what means He chooses to do it, we can be confident in the basic truths given in Scripture. It is the BOOK that sets Christian's mind in motion, revealing his guilt and driving him to find relief from it. And it is the same BOOK that offers us hope and shows us how to find it.

Session 1: Video Notes

1. *"I saw a man with a great* <u>burden</u> *on his back."*
   What is the burden, and who else carries one whether it is visible or not?

   "My guilt has overwhelmed me like a ***burden*** *too heavy to bear"* (Psalm 38:4).

   "If we claim to be without sin, we deceive ourselves and the truth is not in us" (1 John 1:8).

   The burden is the guilt of <u>sin</u>, and <u>everyone</u> carries it.

2. CHRISTIAN: *"Our city is going to be destroyed by fire, and we're all going to* _die_*...unless I find a way for us to* _escape_*."*

   "Our God is a God who saves; from the Sovereign LORD comes ***escape*** *from death"* (Psalm 68:20).

3. WIFE: *"It sounds* _crazy_*. I want you to stop reading this book. It's fairy tales...it's not real. We are perfectly* _safe_ *here."*

   "While people are saying, 'Peace and ***safety,'*** *destruction will come on them suddenly, as labor pains on a pregnant woman, and they will not escape"* (1 Thessalonians 5:3).

4. In this collision of worldviews, if one is true, the other, of necessity, is _false_. If judgment is coming, we are not safe. If the book is _true_, we dare not _ignore_ it.

   "Jesus answered, 'I am the way and the ***truth*** *and the life. No one comes to the Father except through me'"* (John 14:6).

   "How shall we escape if we ***ignore*** *such a great salvation?"* (Hebrews 2:3)?

5. CHRISTIAN: *"No one in this* _world_ *can get rid of this burden." He doesn't have a solution, but he recognizes that the solution has to be supernatural.*

   "The next day John saw Jesus coming toward him and said, 'Look, the Lamb of God, who takes away the sin of the world'" (John 1:29)!

6. *"His family would not listen to him. They refused to open their eyes to the* _truth_*. Like so many, they were* _blinded_ *by the things of this world."*

   "The god of this age has ***blinded*** *the minds of unbelievers, so that they cannot see the light of the gospel of the glory of Christ, who is the image of God"* (2 Corinthians 4:4).

7. CHRISTIAN: *"I am not ready to* _die_*."*

   "Man is destined to ***die*** *once, and after that to face judgment"* (Hebrews 9:27).

8. EVANGELIST: *"With all the evil in the world, wouldn't it be a good thing to get away from it all?" The thought had some appeal, but Christian knew he wasn't* _ready_ *to die.*

   "So you also must be ***ready****, because the Son of Man will come at an hour when you do not expect Him"* (Matthew 24:44).

   Think about it: Are you ready to die?

9. EVANGELIST: *"If you look hard enough, you'll see a shining* _light_*. Run to it."*

   "Your word is a lamp to my feet and a ***light*** *for my path"* (Psalm 119:105).

   "I have come into the world as a ***light****, so that no one who believes in me should stay in darkness"* (John 12:46).

   "If we walk in the ***light****, as He is in the* ***light****, we have fellowship with one another, and the blood of Jesus, his Son, purifies us from all sin"* (1 John 1:7).

10. EVANGELIST: *"And when you get there, you'll* <u>*find*</u> *the gate."*

"You will seek me and ***find*** *me when you seek me with all your heart"* (Jeremiah 29:13).

11. CHRISTIAN (SAYS TO OBSTINATE AND PLIABLE): *"Listen with your* <u>*hearts*</u>*. You know what I'm saying is true."*

"For it is with your ***heart*** *that you believe and are justified, and it is with your mouth that you confess and are saved"* (Romans 10:10).

12. When Christian gets stuck in the river and needs a hand, Pliable is quick to help out. **T or F**

13. Help appears out of nowhere and pulls Christian out of the water.

"Are not all angels ministering spirits sent to serve those who will inherit salvation" (Hebrews 1:14)?

Session 1: Discussion Questions

Consider the supplied Scriptures as you formulate answers.

1. What would you like to discuss from this video segment?

2. Christian tells Obstinate and Pliable to listen with their hearts. Does listening with your heart mean you abandon logic? How would you describe the difference between listening with your head versus your heart?

   ["Head" and "heart" are somewhat ambiguous terms, since some verses describe the heart of fallen man as deceitful and wicked. The meaning in this instance is discerning the difference between what our self-serving logic says versus our God-directed conscience. God does not require us to be illogical; He just knows that we naturally use (or abuse) our logic to manipulate the parts of His revealed truth that we don't like. Our heart (conscience), however, continues to fight against manipulation.]

3. Describe a time in your life when Help came out of nowhere and got you back on the path.

4. Discuss the significance of Christian's question and Help's answer:

CHRISTIAN: "Why isn't the path more clearly marked or better maintained?"

HELP: "Sin. Those pipes are full of it…fear and countless discouraging thoughts…it all ends up right there" (pointing to the path covered by water).

[The path is clear. People deliberately attempt to obscure the truth to hide their own disobedience (sin). God will give more light (direction) to everyone who honestly asks for it.]

"The wrath of God is being revealed from heaven against all the godlessness and wickedness of men who suppress the truth by their wickedness, since what may be known about God is plain to them, because God has made it plain to them. For since the creation of the world God's invisible qualities—His eternal power and divine nature—have been clearly seen, being understood from what has been made, so that men are without excuse" (Romans 1:18-20).

5. Discuss Christian's decision to leave his family to take the path of truth.

   "If anyone comes to me and does not hate his father and mother, his wife and children, his brothers and sisters—yes, even his own life—he cannot be my disciple" (Luke 14:26).

   How can we understand what Jesus meant by this? How does it relate to Christian's choice?

   [This is an example of Jesus using hyperbole—a common form of exaggeration to make a logical point. It does not mean that we are to literally hate our families or our own life. It means that the priority of following Christ must be so absolute that there is no competition from any other value in life. We choose absolute loyalty to Him and trust Him to protect everything else of value.]

Application

What will you start doing, stop doing, or do differently this week in light of what you have seen or heard in this session?

SCRIPTURE TO MEMORIZE

"Watch out! Be on your guard against all kinds of greed; a man's life does not consist in the abundance of his possessions."
Luke 12:15

Dig Deeper and Learn More

Each session contains optional exercises you may do on your own that will help you learn and apply truths from The Pilgrim's Progress. They include a Scripture to memorize and some questions to answer.

1. Recall Evangelist's comment: "If you look hard enough, you'll see a shining light. Run to it." Meditate on the significance of these verses and write a brief response to each one.

   "Your word is a lamp to my feet and a light for my path" (Psalm 119:105).

   "I have come into the world as a light, so that no one who believes in me should stay in darkness" (John 12:46).

   "If we walk in the light, as he is in the light, we have fellowship with one another, and the blood of Jesus, His Son, purifies us from all sin" (1 John 1:7).

2. Recall this dialogue between Christian and Obstinate, and write a personal response for each remark.

OBSTINATE: "You've got everything a person could ever want in this world…a life of luxury."

"Watch out! Be on your guard against all kinds of greed; a man's life does not consist in the abundance of his possessions" (Luke 12:15).

CHRISTIAN: "It's a façade. Come with me and you'll experience real life, real joy. Nothing will compare to what you'll be rewarded with if you follow this path faithfully to the end."

"No eye has seen, no ear has heard, no mind has conceived what God has prepared for those who love him" (1 Corinthians 2:9).

Session 2: Not All Roads Lead to Heaven

"But small is the gate and narrow the road that leads to life, and only a few find it."
Matthew 7:14

Introduction

In the first part of the video, Christian makes the decision to leave everything behind, including the family he loves more than his own life. Motivated by the desire to save them as well as himself, he begins his journey toward the gate. He is convinced that his new destination is real and that it makes everything else secondary.

But the journey isn't easy. When he gets stuck in the Swamp of Despond and is forsaken by his friend, Pliable, he cries out for help. Just when it seems that all hope is lost, Help appears and rescues him.

It would almost make you think Someone was watching. Someone who cared. Someone with a perfect sense of timing—early enough to save him but not too early to keep him from stretching his faith. Someone who is training him to turn panic into trust. And that's where we pick up now.

SESSION 2: VIDEO NOTES

1. HELP: *"But the King has provided a* way out*. You just stay on the path; you're going to be just fine."*

   "No temptation has seized you except what is common to man. And God is faithful; He will not let you be tempted beyond what you can bear. But when you are tempted, He will also provide a ***way out*** *so that you can stand up under it"* (1 Corinthians 10:13).

2. Christian answers Worldly Wise's warning about the dangers ahead if he continues on the path: "Well, I'd rather face all those dangers and more than to carry this throughout my life." What is Christian referring to? Guilt .

   "O my God, I am too ashamed and disgraced to lift up my face to you, my God, because our sins are higher than our heads and our ***guilt*** *has reached to the heavens"* (Ezra 9:6).

3. MR. WORLDLY WISE: "There's a town called Morality ...ask for Mr. Legality. He's an expert at getting rid of burdens like yours."

   "Man is not justified by observing the law, but by faith in Jesus Christ" (Galatians 2:16).

4. EVANGELIST: "Every sin can be forgiven . Just have faith and believe."

   "Praise the LORD, O my soul, and forget not all His benefits—who ***forgives*** *all your sins and heals all your diseases, who redeems your life from the pit and crowns you with love and compassion"*
   (Psalm 103:2-4).

5. EVANGELIST: "Mr. Worldly Wise...led you off the right path... Narrow is the gate that leads to life, and there are few that find it."

   "But small is the gate and ***narrow*** *the road that leads to life, and only a* ***few*** *find it"* (Matthew 7:14).

   Think about it: Have you ever been like Mr. Worldly Wise, thinking that God's acceptance of us is based on our own fabricated version of our acceptability? Our excuses?

6. EVANGELIST: "Mr. Worldly Wise wanted you to be offended at what Christ did at the cross. The King of Glory Himself said that 'He that will save his life will lose it, but he that seeks after the Holy One will save it.'"

   "Whoever wants to save his life will ***lose*** *it, but whoever loses his life for Me and for the gospel will* ***save*** *it"* (Mark 8:35).

7. EVANGELIST: "Mr. Worldly Wise wanted you to be bound to the law so that you would die in your sins and not make it into heaven."

   "I told you that you would die in your sins; if you do not believe that I am the one I claim to be, you will indeed ***die*** *in your* ***sins****"* (John 8:24).

8. GOOD WILL (INSIDE THE GATE): "We never turn anyone away from that gate no matter what their past sins may have been."

   "All that the Father gives me will come to me, and whoever comes to me I will never drive ***away****"* (John 6:37).

   "Everyone who believes in Him receives forgiveness of ***sins*** *through His name"* (Acts 10:43).

9. GOOD WILL: "When you reach the place of deliverance, that burden will fall off by itself."

   "Do not be afraid. Stand firm and you will see the ***deliverance*** *the LORD will bring you today"* (Exodus 14:13).

10. GOOD WILL: "He will tell you great and mighty things which you do not know."

"Call unto me, and I will answer thee, and show thee ***great*** *and* ***mighty*** *things, which thou knowest not"* (Jeremiah 33:3, KJV).

*"**Great** are your purposes and **mighty** are your deeds. Your eyes are open to all the ways of men; you reward everyone according to his conduct and as his deeds deserve"* (Jeremiah 32:19).

*"How **great** are His signs, how **mighty** His wonders! His kingdom is an eternal kingdom; His dominion endures from generation to generation"* (Daniel 4:3).

11. WOMAN IN THE THIRD ROOM OF THE INTERPRETER'S HOUSE: "He called the whole earth to stand before him, and then he told his army to clear the threshing floor, gather the wheat into the barn, but to throw the chaff into the lake of fire."

*"He will clear His threshing floor, gathering His **wheat** into the barn and burning up the **chaff** with unquenchable fire"* (Matthew 3:12).

12. "Many were carried away into the clouds. I was left behind."

*"That is how it will be at the coming of the Son of Man. Two men will be in the field; one will be taken and the other **left**. Two women will be grinding with a hand mill; one will be taken and the other **left**"* (Mark 24:39-41).

13. "I tried to hide…all my sins flashed before my eyes, and I knew I was guilty, and there was nothing I could do or say to change anything."

"They called to the mountains and the rocks, "Fall on us and ***hide*** *us from the face of Him who sits on the throne and from the wrath of the Lamb!"* (Revelation 6:16).

14. "Hell is real. And that's where I'm going."

"For if God did not spare angels when they sinned, but sent them to ***hell****, putting them into gloomy dungeons to be held for judgment; if He did not spare the ancient world when He brought the flood on its ungodly people, but protected Noah, a preacher of righteousness, and seven others; if He condemned the cities of Sodom and Gomorrah by burning them to ashes, and made them an example of what is going to happen to the ungodly; and if He rescued Lot, a righteous man, who was distressed by the filthy lives of lawless men (for that righteous man, living among them day after day, was tormented in his righteous soul by the lawless deeds he saw and heard)— if this is so, then the Lord knows how to rescue godly men from trials and to hold the unrighteous for the day of judgment, while continuing their punishment"* (2 Peter 2:4-9).

SESSION 2: DISCUSSION QUESTIONS

Consider the supplied Scriptures as you formulate answers.

1. What would you like to discuss from this video segment?

2. Mr. Worldly Wise: "Evangelist told you to follow this path? I should have known. He has no idea what he's talking about...I've got the solution. Instead of facing danger, you'll have an easy path."

   How does this approach mimic Satan's temptation of Eve (and nearly every temptation since then)?

   - It distorts the truth in an attempt to destroy its credibility.
   - It leads you to believe you've been mistreated or cheated.
   - It offers an alternative that sounds better, but is always a dead end.

   "Did God really say, 'You must not eat from any tree in the garden'?... You will not surely die,' the serpent said to the woman. 'For God knows that when you eat of it your eyes will be opened, and you will be like God, knowing good and evil'" (Genesis 3:4-5).

   [If God's acceptance of us were based on our arguments and excuses, it would lower the standard to benefit the biggest liar. It would exclude none and make Christ's death unnecessary, since each person would be his or her own law. Heaven then, would be horrible, an eternal extension of our corruption. Instead, God excludes everyone by virtue of their sin and then offers forgiveness and transformation to those who want it. We have a choice, and heaven is protected.]

3. Mr. Worldly Wise looks at Christian's burden (guilt of sin) and asks, "How did you get that thing, anyway?"
Christian holds up the book: "By reading this."
How can reading the Bible result in a burden of guilt?

[The light of God's Word exposes our sin, bringing an awareness of guilt. As painful as this is, it is necessary to drive us to find the relief that can come only through God's forgiveness by grace through faith.]

"Everyone who does evil hates the light, and will not come into the light for fear that his deeds will be exposed. But whoever lives by the truth comes into the light, so that it may be seen plainly that what he has done has been done through God" (John 3:20-21).

4. Discuss the symbolism of the dangers of Mt. Sinai ("Fire Mountain") en route to the town of Morality. Why was it no solution?

[Mt. Sinai is where God gave Moses the Ten Commandments. The mountain's dangers symbolize the fact that God's good law condemns because no one is good enough to perfectly maintain it.]

"All have sinned and fall short of the glory of God" (Romans 3:23).

"Therefore no one will be declared righteous in his sight by observing the law; rather, through the law we become conscious of sin" (Romans 3:20).

That is why "The righteous will live by faith" (Romans 1:17).

5. Mr. Legality (in the town of Morality) is said to be an expert at getting rid of guilt. What are some common defenses people use to excuse themselves?

    - If there's no law against it, it must be okay.
    - The law has a flaw. Here's my loophole.
    - The law was intended to stop serious abuse. It doesn't mind a little bending.
    - Look at so and so…I'm not that bad.
    - The law doesn't apply to me because I'm one of the good guys.
    - There's an exception to every rule—laws were made to be broken.
    - It's only wrong if I get caught.
    - As long as I'm willing to pay the consequences, I can break any law I want.
    - This law is stupid!

Application

What will you start doing, stop doing, or do differently this week in light of what you have seen or heard in this session?

SCRIPTURE TO MEMORIZE

"No temptation has seized you except what is common to man. And God is faithful; He will not let you be tempted beyond what you can bear. But when you are tempted, He will also provide a way out so that you can stand up under it"

1 Corinthians 10:13.

Dig Deeper and Learn More

Each session contains optional exercises you may do on your own that will help you learn and apply truths from The Pilgrim's Progress. They include a Scripture to memorize and some questions to answer.

1. The following two passages could be interpreted to be contradictory, but they are not. The fact that the first one is from the Old Testament and the second one is from the New Testament is irrelevant. In what ways are they simultaneously true?

   "Great are your purposes and mighty are your deeds. Your eyes are open to all the ways of men; you reward everyone according to his conduct and as his deeds deserve" (Jeremiah 32:19).

   "He saved us, not because of righteous things we had done, but because of His mercy" (Titus 3:5).

   - Are rewards and salvation the same thing? Consider the important distinction between rewards for behavior and salvation by faith.

   - Think of examples of earthly rewards (both good and bad) that God gives.

- The Bible, without going into much detail, informs us that there are also heavenly rewards. Consider, for instance *1 Corinthians 3:12-15; 1 Peter 5:1-4; 1 Corinthians 9:24-25; Matthew 18:4.*

Since God's all-knowing judgment will reveal every thought, motive, word and deed—regardless of our redemption and entrance into heaven—how important is it to live daily for His approval? How do you plan to do it?

2. Recall the room with the dust of original sin. "The man sweeping the room represents the law, which instead of cleansing the heart, only gives sin its strength. The woman who sprinkled the water represents the gospel, which is able to overcome sin in our lives. Once the heart is clean, it's fit for the King of Glory to come in and live." What do you think the Interpreter means when he says the law gives sin its strength?

[Since the nature of sin is to distort and deceive, it needs something good to work on. The law, which reveals God's character, is good. The more we understand it, and the more we see the holiness of God, the more we see the impossibility of measuring up. Sin uses the law to accuse us and deceive us into running away from God—just as Adam and Eve hid in the Garden.

God cannot save us through the law because the law always finds us guilty. But He can save us through grace, which declares us not guilty by virtue of God taking our punishment Himself.]

"The sting of death is sin, and the power of sin is the law" (1 Corinthians 15:56).

"For when we were controlled by the sinful nature, the sinful passions aroused by the law were at work in our bodies... What shall we say, then? Is the law sin? Certainly not! Indeed I would not have known what sin was except through the law. For I would not have known what coveting really was if the law had not said, 'Do not covet.' But sin, seizing the opportunity afforded by the commandment, produced in me every kind of covetous desire. For apart from law, sin is dead. Once I was alive apart from law; but when the commandment came, sin sprang to life and I died. I found that the very commandment that was intended to bring life actually brought death.

For sin, seizing the opportunity afforded by the commandment, deceived me, and through the commandment put me to death. So then, the law is holy, and the commandment is holy, righteous and good. Did that which is good, then, become death to me? By no means! But in order that sin might be recognized as sin, it produced death in me through what was good, so that through the commandment sin might become utterly sinful" (Romans 7:5, 7-13).

Session 3: Sin Forgiven, Guilt Released, and Armor for the Journey

"The testing of your faith develops perseverance."
James 1:3

Introduction

Christian has two driving motivations. First, he wants to save himself and his family from the destruction to come. Second, he has an intense need to rid himself of his growing sense of sin. The journey is hard enough without having to lug around such a grotesque burden.

Every time he has left the path for what appeared to be a way to release the burden, he has met with disappointment. Empty promises. Unadvertised dangers.

The Interpreter reveals great and sobering truths to him. The first room shows him the need for the gospel to deal with the pervasive dust of sin. The second room shows him his need for hope and courage to keep moving toward his heavenly goal. The third room shows him the despair of fear and the reality of hell.

Fortified by all of this, he resumes his journey. But the burden is still on his back—bigger and heavier than ever. He knows more, but he has not yet seen his solution and surrendered to it. In God's perfect timing, he will.

Session 3: Video Notes

1. On his knees at the foot of the cross, Christian hears the sound of ropes breaking—the ropes that bound his burden of sin to him. It is just as Good Will had predicted: "When you reach the place of deliverance, that burden will fall off by itself." Christian is set free.

   "He forgave us all our sins, having canceled the written code, with its regulations, that was against us and that stood opposed to us; He took it away, nailing it to the ***cross****"* (Colossians 2:13-14).

   "Then you will know the truth, and the truth will ***set you free****"* (John 8:32).

2. CHRISTIAN: "You have given me rest by your sorrow and life by your death."

"Surely He took up our infirmities and carried our ***sorrows****...He was pierced for our transgressions, He was crushed for our iniquities; the punishment that brought us peace was upon Him, and by His wounds we are healed"* (Isaiah 53:4-5).

3. ANGELS AT THE CROSS: "Study these words, as they will give you strength for the journey."

"Fix these ***words*** *of mine in your hearts and minds; tie them as symbols on your hands and bind them on your foreheads"* (Deuteronomy 11:18).

"Your words have supported those who stumbled; You have ***strengthened*** *faltering knees"* (Job 4:4).

4. At the entrance to the Palace Beautiful, Christian is frightened by statues of lions that roar and threaten to attack. A man comes out and says, "Is your faith so small? They are here to test your faith. If you stay on the path, you'll be fine."

"Then Peter got down out of the boat, walked on the water and came toward Jesus. But when he saw the wind, he was afraid and, beginning to sink, cried out, 'Lord, save me!'

Immediately Jesus reached out His hand and caught him. "You of little ***faith****," He said, "why did you doubt?" And when they climbed into the boat, the wind died down"* (Matthew 14:29-32).

"The testing of your ***faith*** *develops perseverance"* (James 1:3).

5. A few days later, Christian is shown a great room that holds many artifacts and weapons to strengthen the faithful on their journey to heaven. Porter: "It's amazing how God uses ordinary people and ordinary things to accomplish great miracles."

   "Brothers, think of what you were when you were called. Not many of you were wise by human standards; not many were influential; not many were of noble birth" (1 Corinthians 1:26).

   "But we have this treasure in jars of clay to show that this all-surpassing power is from God and not from us" (2 Corinthians 4:7).

6. PORTER: "Samson used this jawbone to defeat an entire army all by himself. And this is the sling and stone that David used to defeat Goliath at Gath."

   "Some trust in chariots and some in horses, but we trust in the name of the LORD our God"—[said by David, who defeated Goliath] (Psalm 20:7).

7. Christian is given armor to protect him on his journey.

   *"Put on the full **armor** of God so that you can take your stand against the devil's schemes. For our struggle is not against flesh and blood, but against the rulers, against the authorities, against the powers of this dark world and against the spiritual forces of evil in the heavenly realms. Therefore put on the full **armor** of God, so that when the day of evil comes, you may be able to stand your ground, and after you have done everything, to stand. Stand firm then, with the belt of truth buckled around your waist, with the breastplate of righteousness in place, and with your feet fitted with the readiness that comes from the gospel of peace. In addition to all this, take up the shield of faith, with which you can extinguish all*

the flaming arrows of the evil one. Take the helmet of salvation and the sword of the Spirit, which is the word of God" (Ephesians 6:11-17).

Think about it: Are you using the "full armor of God" or are you relying on your own strength? Do you understand who the enemy really is?

8. Christian would soon need his new sword and armor against the mighty demon, Apollyon.

   CHRISTIAN TO APOLLYON: "Your wages are too great for any man, for the wages of sin is death."

   *"For the wages of sin is **death**, but the gift of God is eternal life in Christ Jesus our Lord"* (Romans 6:23).

9. APOLLYON: "I promise to pay you handsomely if you turn and go back to my country."

   CHRISTIAN: "I've given myself to the King of Kings. How can I possibly go back now?"

   APOLLYON: "There are many who have chosen to follow your king. But they come back to me."

   *"They promise them freedom, while they themselves are slaves of depravity—for a man is a slave to whatever has mastered him. If they have escaped the corruption of the world by knowing our Lord and Savior Jesus Christ and are again entangled in it and overcome, they are worse off at the end than they were at the beginning. It would have been better for them not to have known the way of righteousness, than to have known it and then to turn their backs on the sacred command that was passed on to them. Of them the proverbs are true: 'A dog returns to its vomit,' and, 'A sow that is washed goes **back** to her wallowing in the mud'"* (2 Peter 2:19-22).

10. CHRISTIAN TO APOLLYON: "The trials and tribulations are to test and strengthen our faith. And those that die will receive great rewards when my Prince comes in his glory."

"Do not be afraid of what you are about to suffer. I tell you, the devil will put some of you in prison to ***test*** *you, and you will suffer persecution for ten days. Be faithful, even to the point of death, and I will give you the crown of life"* (Revelation 2:10).

"We ought always to thank God for you, brothers, and rightly so, because your faith is growing more and more, and the love every one of you has for each other is increasing. Therefore, among God's churches we boast about your perseverance and faith in all the persecutions and ***trials*** *you are enduring. All this is evidence that God's judgment is right, and as a result you will be counted worthy of the kingdom of God, for which you are suffering"* (2 Thessalonians 1:3-5).

11. APOLLYON TO CHRISTIAN: "You've already been unfaithful to him from the very beginning."

CHRISTIAN: "How?"

APOLLYON: "You almost drowned in the swamp of Despond. You wandered off the path to get rid of your burden. Fear grips you often, and still you're considering turning back."

CHRISTIAN: "That's true and much more. But the Prince I serve and love is ready to forgive when I repent of my sins."

*"****Repent*** *and be baptized, every one of you, in the name of Jesus Christ for the* ***forgiveness*** *of your sins"* (Acts 2:38).

Think about it: Have you recognized your own unfaithfulness and dealt with it?

12. HEALING HAND: "The Lord has sent me with leaves from the tree of life that will heal you and give you strength for the journey."

"On each side of the river stood the ***tree of life****, bearing twelve crops of fruit, yielding its fruit every month. And the leaves of the tree are for the healing of the nations"* (Revelation 22:2).

Session 3: Discussion Questions

Consider the supplied Scriptures as you formulate answers.

1. What would you like to discuss from this video segment?

2. When the angels at the cross gave Christian the scroll, they said, "Study these words as they will give you strength for the journey." Discuss your personal experience with the power of God's Word to give you strength.

   "How can a young man keep his way pure? By living according to your word...I have hidden your word in my heart that I might not sin against you" (Psalm 119:9, 11).

3. In Palace Beautiful, after showing Christian many of the items used in the miracles of the Bible, Porter says, "It's amazing how God uses ordinary people and ordinary things to accomplish great miracles." How has God used ordinary things and people in your life? Why do you think he chooses to work that way?

   "But God chose the foolish things of the world to shame the wise; God chose the weak things of the world to shame the strong. He chose the lowly things of this world and the despised things—and the things that are not—to nullify the things that are, so that no one may boast before Him. It is because of Him that you are in Christ Jesus, who has become for us wisdom from God—that is, our righteousness, holiness and redemption. Therefore, as it is written: 'Let him who boasts boast in the Lord'" (1 Corinthians 1:27-31).

4. When Apollyon says to Christian: "You've already been unfaithful to him [your Prince] from the very beginning," he is accusing him of the very thing he is tempting him to do. How have you experienced Satan using this pattern to try to defeat you?

   "Then I heard a loud voice in heaven say: 'Now have come the salvation and the power and the kingdom of our God, and the authority of His Christ. For the accuser of our brothers, who accuses them before our God day and night, has been hurled down'" (Revelation 12:10).

5. Christian learns from experience that our trials and tribulations are to test and strengthen our faith. How have you experienced this?

   "Consider it pure joy, my brothers, whenever you face trials of many kinds, because you know that the testing of your faith develops perseverance. Perseverance must finish its work so that you may be mature and complete, not lacking anything" (James 1:2-4).

Application

What will you start doing, stop doing, or do differently this week in light of what you have seen or heard in this session?

SCRIPTURE TO MEMORIZE

"For the wages of sin is death, but the gift of God is eternal life in Christ Jesus our Lord" Romans 6:23.

Dig Deeper and Learn More

Each session contains optional exercises you may do on your own that will help you learn and apply truths from The Pilgrim's Progress. They include a Scripture to memorize and some questions to answer.

1. Using Ephesians 6:11-17 (printed earlier in Study Note #7), list the various pieces of armor.
   - Which of these are you using regularly?
   - Which of these do you need to focus on?
   - What will you do to ensure that you make better use of the armor God has given you?

2. *First Chronicles 21* is a fascinating story of David learning an important lesson—the hard way. When he later said (in *Psalm 20:7*), "Some trust in chariots and some in horses, but we trust in the name of the LORD our God," he was expressing a trust that he had not always maintained.

Read *1 Chronicles 21* and write some brief responses to parallels in your own life.

- David gives in to the temptation to put his trust in the strength of his armies.
- David fails to listen to counsel from Joab.
- David feels convicted about his sin and confesses to God.
- God forgives him, but disciplines him with the consequences of his disobedience.
- Because David is the king/leader, the consequences also extend to the people.
- David shows his sincerity by saying, *"I will not take for the LORD what is yours, or sacrifice a burnt offering that costs me nothing" (1 Chronicles 21:24).*

3. When Apollyon accuses Christian of being unfaithful to his prince, Christian admits it and then says, "But the Prince I serve and love is ready to forgive when I repent of my sins."

   Repentance is more than confession, more than remorse; it is turning away from, making a change in direction. Read *Psalm 51* to see a picture of the confession and repentance of a broken man. David, a man after God's own heart, failed many times, but he never stopped pursuing God.

   List the important truths that jump out at you from *Psalm 51.*

   Meditate on *Psalm 51* and make it your pattern when you realize you have sinned.

SESSION 4: THE POWER OF THE WORD

"Be strong and very courageous. Be careful to obey all the law my servant Moses gave you; do not turn from it to the right or to the left, that you may be successful wherever you go."
Joshua 1:7

INTRODUCTION

Christian has finally gotten relief from his enormous burden of guilt. While on his knees at the cross, the burden falls from his back and evaporates.

But his other objective—to reach the Celestial City and help his family escape the destruction to come—still lies ahead of him. So do many trials and tribulations. Angels at the cross give him God's Word and tell him to study it for strength.

Almost immediately his faith is tested, and he learns the importance of staying on the path. After learning more about faith during his stay in the Palace Beautiful, he puts on his new armor and continues the journey.

Apollyon nearly defeats Christian with accusations that test his faithfulness to his new Prince. At the crucial time, Christian is able to use *"the sword of the Spirit, which is the word of God" (Ephesians 6:17)* to defeat Apollyon. The wounds he has suffered in the process are serious, but God sends Healing Hand with leaves from the Tree of Life to heal him and give him strength.

Session 4: Video Notes

1. With renewed strength, Christian resumes his journey—this time into the Valley of the Shadow of Death. With mortal dangers all around, he puts his sword away and defends himself by quoting Scripture.

   *"Even though I walk through the valley of the shadow of **death**, I will fear no evil, for you are with me; your rod and your staff, they comfort me"* (Psalm 23:4).

2. After safely passing through the Valley of the Shadow of Death, Christian prays for God to give him a companion for the journey. His prayer is answered as Faithful, an old <u>friend</u> from the city of Destruction, comes into sight.

   "Two are better than one, because they have a good return for their work: If one falls down, his ***friend*** *can help him up. But pity the man who falls and has no one to help him up* (Ecclesiastes 4:9-10)"

3. FAITHFUL: "Everybody's talking about how the whole town is going to be consumed by fire from heaven."

   CHRISTIAN: "Where is everyone?"

   FAITHFUL: "They talked themselves out of believing it would happen."

   "From this time many of His disciples turned back and no longer followed Him. 'You do not want to leave too, do you?' Jesus asked the Twelve" (John 6:66-67).

   "We have come to share in Christ if we hold firmly till the end the confidence we had at first" (Hebrews 3:14).

4. FAITHFUL: "At the entrance of the City Gate, I met Wanton, the seductress. She was absolutely gorgeous, and she knew exactly what to say. I resisted her temptation by remembering the Proverb, 'Her feet go down to death; her steps take hold on hell.'"

   "Her feet go down to ***death;*** *her steps take hold on* ***hell****"* (Proverbs 5:5, KJV).

   "For a man's ways are in full view of the LORD, and He examines all his paths. The evil deeds of a wicked man ensnare him; the cords of his sin hold him fast. He will die for lack of discipline, led astray by his own great folly" (Proverbs 5:21-23).

5. FAITHFUL: "But I'll be honest with you. There are times I find myself thinking about her, wanting her. Lord knows I wish I'd never met her."

   "When tempted, no one should say, 'God is tempting me.' For God cannot be tempted by evil, nor does he tempt anyone; but each one is tempted when, by his own evil desire, he is dragged away and enticed. Then, after desire has conceived, it gives birth to sin; and sin, when it is full-grown, gives birth to death" (James 1:13-15).

6. FAITHFUL: "I met a guy by the name of Adam the First from the town of deceit...he offered me his three beautiful daughters in marriage: Lust of the Flesh, Lust of the Eyes, and the Pride of Life."

   "For all that is in the world, the lust of the ***flesh****, and the lust of the* ***eyes****, and the* ***pride*** *of life, is not of the Father, but is of the world"* (1 John 2:16).

7. FAITHFUL: "I saw written on his forehead, 'Put off the old man and his deeds.' It was like my eyes were opened. No matter what this man told me, no matter how much he flattered me, I knew his goal was to get me to his house so that he could sell me into a life of slavery."

"...put off the old man with his ***deeds****"* (Colossians 3:9).

"It is for freedom that Christ has set us free. Stand firm, then, and do not let yourselves be burdened again by a yoke of ***slavery****"* (Galatians 5:1).

Think about it: The lust of the flesh (illicit sensual pleasures), the lust of the eyes (greed), and the pride of life (elevating self above God, the temporal above the eternal)—all of these naturally tempt us. If we give in to them, they enslave us. Like addictive drugs, they ruin our lives and weaken our ability to leave them behind.

8. EVANGELIST: "Now, above all, guard your heart against the evil desires of the world because the heart itself is desperately wicked."

"Above all else, guard your ***heart****"* (Proverbs 4:23).

"The heart is deceitful above all things, and desperately ***wicked****"* (Jeremiah 17:9).

9. EVANGELIST: "Remember, you've got all the powers of heaven and earth on your side."

"His divine ***power*** *has given us everything we need for life and godliness through our knowledge of Him who called us by His own glory and goodness"* (2 Peter 1:3).

10. EVANGELIST: "One or both of you will be killed for your testimony of our Lord Jesus Christ. But be faithful, even to death, and the King will give you a crown."

"Others were tortured and refused to be released, so that they might gain a better resurrection. Some faced jeers and flogging, while still others were chained and put in prison. They were stoned; they were sawed in two; they were put to death by the sword. They went about in sheepskins and goatskins, destitute, persecuted and mistreated—the world was not worthy of them. They wandered in deserts and mountains, and in caves and holes in the ground. These were all commended for their faith, yet none of them received what had been promised. God had planned something better for us so that only together with us would they be made perfect" (Hebrews 11:35-40).

"Do not be afraid of what you are about to suffer. I tell you, the devil will put some of you in prison to test you, and you will suffer persecution for ten days. Be faithful, even to the point of death, and I will give you the crown of life" (Revelation 2:10).

11. EVANGELIST: "Stay the course. God is faithful to the end."

*"God is **faithful;** He will not let you be tempted beyond what you can bear. But when you are tempted, He will also provide a way out so that you can stand up under it"* (1 Corinthians 10:13).

*"And surely I am with you always, to the very **end"*** (Matthew 28:20).

12. Christian and Faithful would not buy anything from the merchants of Vanity Fair. Instead, they tried to share the good news of the gospel. But the town's people grew angry and turned on them.

"If you belonged to the world, it would love you as its own. As it is, you do not belong to the world, but I have chosen you out of the world. That is why the world hates you" (John 15:19).

13. FAITHFUL: "Jesus said that 'I am the truth and the life; that no man shall come to the Father except through me.'"

"Jesus answered, 'I am the way and the ***truth*** *and the* ***life****. No one comes to the Father except through me'"* (John 14:6).

14. FAITHFUL: "Any religion that is built on faith in one's self and not on faith in God is worthless."

"Where, then, is boasting? It is excluded. On what principle? On that of observing the law? No, but on that of faith…there is only one God, who will justify the circumcised by faith and the uncircumcised through that same faith" (Romans 3:27-30).

15. FAITHFUL (BEING LED TO EXECUTION): "I'll see you in the heavenly kingdom!"

CHRISTIAN: "Be strong, Faithful!"

"Have I not commanded you? Be ***strong*** *and courageous. Do not be terrified; do not be discouraged, for the LORD your God will be with you wherever you go"* (Joshua 1:9).

Session 4: Discussion Questions

Consider the supplied Scriptures as you formulate answers.

1. What would you like to discuss from this video segment?

2. After resisting the temptation of Wanton, the seductress, Faithful is still plagued by memories and desires. He says, "I wish I'd never met her." Discuss how easy it is to rationalize curiosity and open a dangerous door that never should be cracked open. How can we gain the wisdom and discernment to preempt dangerous attractions by never giving them a chance to become full-blown temptations?

   "The prudent see danger and take refuge [flee from it], but the simple keep going and suffer for it" (Proverbs 22:7).

   "Keep to a path far from her, do not go near the door of her house" (Proverbs 5:8).

3. Discuss: God does not prohibit us from doing anything unless it is hurtful to ourselves or others. True or False?

If you answer "False," think of (and discuss) an example.

If you answer "True," discuss our surprising tendency to resent God's commands and feel as though He is holding out on us or restricting our freedom with no good reason.

"They are a nation without sense, there is no discernment in them. If only they were wise and would understand this and discern what their end will be" (Deuteronomy 32:28-29)!

"Open my eyes that I may see wonderful things in your law" (Psalm 119:18).

"Give me understanding, and I will keep your law and obey it with all my heart" (Psalm 119:34).

"The earth is filled with your love, O LORD; teach me your decrees" (Psalm 119:64).

4. The townspeople of Vanity Fair illustrated the hatred Jesus spoke of in John 15:19: "…you do not belong to the world, but I have chosen you out of the world. That is why the world hates you."

   Discuss the following statements and their implications.

   - "I feel hated by the world because of my stand for Christ."
   - "I don't feel hated by the world. I think the world is much more godly than it was during the time of Christ, so we are all pretty similar these days."
   - "I don't feel hated by the world. I think people are still living for themselves more than for God, but if I am honest, I have to say I have identified more with them than with living and proclaiming God's truth."

   "There will be terrible times in the last days. People will be lovers of themselves, lovers of money, boastful, proud, abusive, disobedient to their parents, ungrateful, unholy, without love, unforgiving, slanderous, without self-control, brutal, not lovers of the good, treacherous, rash, conceited, lovers of pleasure rather than lovers of God—having a form of godliness but denying its power. Have nothing to do with them" (2 Timothy 3:1-5).

5. Faithful quotes Jesus in *John 14:6* saying, *"I am the way and the truth and the life. No one comes to the Father except through me."* In an age that wants to believe that all roads lead to the same destination, the message of Pilgrim's Progress is that the path is narrow and exclusive.

   Discuss:

   - Does 2 + 2 really = 4 or should it be allowed to equal any number we choose?
   - Is God's Word a different kind of truth—too ambiguous to know with any certainty? Was Jesus mistaken when He said what He did in John 14:6?
   - How might we inadvertently make the simple truth ambiguous in an attempt to make it more acceptable to people?
   - How can we graciously proclaim the truth as stated in the Bible and let God deal with people's response?
   - Can we trust God to enable people to accept what may feel like hard truth?
   - How can we grow in our faithfulness to share the truth in a way that is always clearly motivated by God's love and grace?

APPLICATION

What will you start doing, stop doing, or do differently this week in light of what you have seen or heard in this session?

SCRIPTURE TO MEMORIZE

"Jesus answered, 'It is written: 'Man does not live on bread alone, but on every word that comes from the mouth of God' "
Matthew 4:4.

Dig Deeper and Learn More

Each session contains optional exercises you may do on your own that will help you learn and apply truths from The Pilgrim's Progress. They include a Scripture to memorize and some questions to answer.

1. When Christian was entering the Shadow of the Valley of Death, he pulled out his sword, but then put it away, choosing a stronger weapon. Quoting Scripture, he made his way safely through the treacherous valley. Read *Matthew 4:1-11* and notice the pattern set by Jesus. How did He respond to every temptation?

   "Jesus answered, 'It is written: 'Man does not live on bread alone, but on every word that comes from the mouth of God'" (Matthew 4:4).

   When you are under the gun of temptation or danger, are you able to quote verses that apply?

   Both Joshua and David knew the secret of success.

"Be strong and very courageous. Be careful to obey all the law my servant Moses gave you; do not turn from it to the right or to the left, that you may be successful wherever you go" (Joshua 1:7).

"Then you will have success if you are careful to observe the decrees and laws that the LORD gave Moses for Israel. Be strong and courageous. Do not be afraid or discouraged" (1 Chronicles 22:13).

They spoke specifically about the law of Moses because that was the only Scripture they had. We have the benefit of the rest of the Old Testament and all of the New Testament as well. Remember Jesus' words "that we should live 'on every word that comes from the mouth of God" (Matthew 4:4).

Make a list of the temptations, fears and discouragements you are most likely to face in coming months. Search for verses that apply most directly to each one and begin to memorize them. These are your most valuable weapons and the "bread" that will sustain you.

2. Take a week to read *Psalm 119* multiple times, noting the high value it places on God's Word.

    - Sense David's longing to know and obey the heart of God.
    - Make a list of verses that speak strongly to your heart.
    - Meditate on these verses throughout the week, asking God to instill in you the same passion David felt for God and His Word.

Session 5: Remembering Past Victories and the Key of Promise

"Let us hold unswervingly to the hope we profess, for He who promised is faithful."
Hebrews 10:23

Introduction

Shortly after receiving healing and strength from leaves of the Tree of Life, Christian faces his most fearful encounter yet—the Valley of the Shadow of Death. He pulls out his sword but then puts it away, choosing a stronger weapon. Quoting Scripture, he makes his way safely through the treacherous valley and then asks God to give him a companion for the journey.

Faithful joins him and describes his encounters with Wanton, the seductress, and Adam the First, who tempts him with the Lust of the Flesh, the Lust of the Eyes, and the Pride of Life. All of these temptations are defeated by the power of remembered Scripture.

Evangelist crosses their path again and encourages them with additional truth from God's word. He also warns, "One or both of you will be killed for your testimony of our Lord Jesus Christ. But be faithful, even to death, and the King will give you a crown. Stay the course. God is faithful to the end."

Christian and Faithful live up to their names in the crucible of an evil courtroom, where Faithful gives a stirring testimony and is sentenced to death. But Faithful takes comfort in knowing that he will beat Christian to the Celestial City.

Session 5: Video Notes

1. As Faithful is being dragged out of the courtroom, the judge sarcastically asks, "Where is your God now, Faithful?"

   *"My tears have been my food day and night, while men say to me all day long, 'Where is your **God**' "* (Psalm 23:4)?

   "The people stood watching, and the rulers even sneered at Him. They said, 'He saved others; let Him save Himself if He is the Christ of God, the Chosen One' " (Luke 23:35).

2. When the torch lights the wood that will burn Faithful to death, he looks out and says, "Forgive them, Father. They don't know what they do."

   "When they came to the place called the Skull, there they crucified Him, along with the criminals—one on His right, the other on His left. Jesus said, 'Father, ***forgive*** *them, for they do not know what they are doing'"* (Luke 23:33-34).

3. Christian escapes before execution and, along with his new companion, Hopeful, is misled from the path by Vain Confidence.

   "For it is we who are the circumcision, we who worship by the Spirit of God, who glory in Christ Jesus, and who put no ***confidence*** *in the flesh"* (Hebrews 3:14).

   Think about it: Are you ever tempted to define your own path, assuming it is as valid as the one defined in the Bible?

4. The giant, Despair, takes Christian and Hopeful to Doubting Castle and imprisons them without food or water. He beats them and provides nothing except tools for them to escape their misery by taking their own lives.

   "We were under great pressure, far beyond our ability to endure, so that we ***despaired*** *even of life"* (2 Corinthians 1:8).

5. Hopeful, as Christian is considering killing himself: "Remember that God is bigger than any giant we may face. We can get through this."

   "Be strong and courageous. Do not be afraid or discouraged because of the king of Assyria and the vast army with him, for there is a greater power with us than with him" (2 Chronicles 32:7).

   "My Father, who has given them to me, is greater than all; no one can snatch them out of my Father's hand" (John 10:29).

   "You, dear children, are from God and have overcome them, because the one who is in you is greater than the one who is in the world" (1 John 4:4).

6. Later, as the Giant, Despair, threatens them again, Hopeful helps Christian remember past victories. "Let us not forget what God has done for us. Let's just wait on Him and see what He will do."

   *"**Remember** how the LORD your God led you all the way in the desert these forty years, to humble you and to test you in order to know what was in your heart, whether or not you would keep His commands"* (1 John 2:16).

   *"We **wait** in hope for the LORD; He is our help and our shield"* (Psalm 33:20).

   *"Be still before the LORD and **wait** patiently for Him; do not fret when men succeed in their ways, when they carry out their wicked schemes"* (Psalm 37:7).

7. HOPEFUL: "I know what we should do…Pray."

   CHRISTIAN: "That's a great idea."

   HOPEFUL: "Something we should've done a long time ago."

   *"And **pray** in the Spirit on all occasions with all kinds of prayers and requests. With this in mind, be alert and always keep on praying"* (Ephesians 6:18).

8. CHRISTIAN (After Rediscovering The Key Around His Neck): "This is the key called Promise, given to me at the cross."

   *"I will give you the **keys** of the kingdom of heaven; whatever you bind on earth will be bound in heaven, and whatever you loose on earth will be loosed in heaven"* (Matthew 16:19).

9. Shepherd explains the unburied men at the bottom of Mt. Error: "They are examples, a warning to those who have lost their way because of the false teaching on the resurrection. Remember that Jesus has risen indeed!"

   *"Their teaching will spread like gangrene. Among them are Hymenaeus and Philetus, who have wandered away from the truth. They say that the **resurrection** has already taken place, and they destroy the faith of some. Nevertheless, God's solid foundation stands firm, sealed with this inscription: 'The Lord knows those who are his'"* (2 Timothy 2:17-19).

   *"Jesus said to her, 'I am the **resurrection** and the life. He who believes in me will live, even though he dies'"* (John 11:25).

   *"With great power the apostles continued to testify to the **resurrection** of the Lord Jesus, and much grace was upon them all"* (Acts 4:33).

10. Shepherd points out men who have been blinded by the Giant, Despair, and forced to grope among the tombs, "thus fulfilling the Proverb, 'A man who strays from the path of understanding comes to rest in the company of the dead.'"

*"A man who **strays** from the path of **understanding** comes to rest in the company of the dead"* (Proverbs 21:16).

Think about it: Despair is the logical conclusion of atheism. Hope, the antidote to despair, requires faith in God to redeem His fallen creation and restore its splendor.

11. SHEPHERD: "Watch yourselves. This is a shortcut to hell. This is for hypocrites."
HOPEFUL: "You mean everyone here was on their way to the Celestial City?"
SHEPHERD: "They believed it until they ended up here."

*"He [Jesus] replied, 'Isaiah was right when he prophesied about you **hypocrites;** as it is written: These people honor me with their lips, but their hearts are far from me' "* (Matthew 28:20).

*"Woe to you, teachers of the law and Pharisees, you **hypocrites!** You travel over land and sea to win a single convert, and when he becomes one, you make him twice as much a son of **hell** as you are"* (Matthew 23:15).

12. SHEPHERD (Pointing): "There, perhaps you can see. Your heart's desire, the gates of the Celestial City, where the King awaits his faithful."

"In my Father's house are many rooms; if it were not so, I would have told you. I am going there to prepare a place for you. And if I go and prepare a place for you, I will come back and take you to be with me that you also may be where I am" (John 14:2-3).

SESSION 5: DISCUSSION QUESTIONS

Consider the supplied Scriptures as you formulate answers.

1. What would you like to discuss from this video segment?

2. Recall the scene where the judge sarcastically asks, "Where is your God now, Faithful?" Discuss the importance of perspective in interpreting the reality of any given moment:

   - The fool, who believes there is no God, sees every request that isn't immediately answered as further proof that God does not exist.

   - The believer who has trained himself to trust God sees unanswered requests as evidence of a better plan—one that God is still in the process of revealing.

   What examples from your own life illustrate that your trust in God is more than mere wishful thinking?

   "In You our fathers put their trust; they trusted and you delivered them. They cried to you and were saved; in you they trusted and were not disappointed" (Psalm 22:4-5).

3. At a crucial time, Hopeful helped Christian remember past victories. "Let us not forget what God has done for us." Why is it so important to remember?

   "No sooner had Gideon died than the Israelites again prostituted themselves to the Baals. They set up Baal-Berith as their god and did not remember the LORD their God, who had rescued them from the hands of all their enemies on every side" (Judges 8:33-34).

   "Then they believed His promises and sang His praise. But they soon forgot what He had done and did not wait for His counsel. In the desert they gave in to their craving; in the wasteland they put God to the test" (Psalm 106:12-14).

4. Hopeful and Christian were in the dungeon for a long time before Hopeful thought about praying. Why do we often treat prayer as the last resort?

   What does this reveal about where our hope and confidence are really placed?

   "Do not be anxious about anything, but in everything, by prayer and petition, with thanksgiving, present your requests to God" (Philippians 4:6).

5. Hopeful and Christian remained in the dungeon until they were nearly dead from starvation and dehydration. In all that time, Christian never thought about the Key of Promise he had been given at the cross. Discuss:

The significance of the promises we have been given by God. Below are a few to start your thinking. What kinds of doors do these promises unlock?

"God is faithful; He will not let you be tempted beyond what you can bear. But when you are tempted, He will also provide a way out so that you can stand up under it" (1 Corinthians 10:13).

"And surely I am with you always, to the very end" (Matthew 28:20).

"Ask and it will be given to you; seek and you will find; knock and the door will be opened to you. For everyone who asks receives; he who seeks finds; and to him who knocks, the door will be opened" (Matthew 7:7-8).

Discuss our tendency to leave these promises unclaimed. How can we develop the habit of remembering and claiming them sooner?

"Your kingdom is an everlasting kingdom, and your dominion endures through all generations. The LORD is faithful to all His promises and loving toward all He has made" (Psalm 145:13).

Application

What will you start doing, stop doing, or do differently this week in light of what you have seen or heard in this session?

SCRIPTURE TO MEMORIZE

"Do not be anxious about anything, but in everything, by prayer and petition, with thanksgiving, present your requests to God" Philippians 4:6.

Dig Deeper and Learn More

Each session contains optional exercises you may do on your own that will help you learn and apply truths from The Pilgrim's Progress. They include a Scripture to memorize and some questions to answer.

1. In addressing hypocrites, Jesus often refers to them as blind guides.

   • Is it possible to have a problem with hypocrisy and be blind to it?

   • Is it possible that you have a tendency toward hypocrisy?

   • How can you protect yourself from becoming hypocritical?

   "Leave them; they are blind guides. If a blind man leads a blind man, both will fall into a pit" (Matthew 15:14).

   "Do nothing out of selfish ambition or vain conceit, but in humility consider others better than yourselves" (Philippians 2:3).

   "Therefore, as God's chosen people, holy and dearly loved, clothe yourselves with compassion, kindness, humility, gentleness and patience" (Colossians 3:12).

   "Who is wise and understanding among you? Let him show it by his good life, by deeds done in the humility that comes from wisdom" (James 3:13).

2. Do a study on the promises of God. You can begin with these verses that describe God's faithfulness to deliver on His promises.

   "God is not a man, that He should lie, nor a son of man, that He should change His mind. Does he speak and then not act? Does He promise and not fulfill" (Numbers 23:19)?

   "Now I am about to go the way of all the earth. You know with all your heart and soul that not one of all the good promises the LORD your God gave you has failed. Every promise has been fulfilled; not one has failed" (Joshua 23:14).

   "My comfort in my suffering is this: Your promise preserves my life" (Psalm 119:50).

   "Yet he did not waver through unbelief regarding the promise of God, but was strengthened in his faith and gave glory to God, being fully persuaded that God had power to do what he had promised" (Romans 4:20-21).

   "Let us hold unswervingly to the hope we profess, for He who promised is faithful" (Hebrews 10:23).

   "Through these He has given us his very great and precious promises, so that through them you may participate in the divine nature and escape the corruption in the world caused by evil desires" (2 Peter 1:4).

   "The Lord is not slow in keeping His promise, as some understand slowness. He is patient with you, not wanting anyone to perish, but everyone to come to repentance" (2 Peter 3:9).

   Then begin searching for actual promises. In addition to the ones listed in Discussion Question #5, here are a few (out of hundreds) to get you started.

   "For God so loved the world that He gave his one and only Son, that whoever believes in Him shall not perish but have eternal life" (John 3:16).

   "In my Father's house are many rooms; if it were not so, I would have told you. I am going there to prepare a place for you. And if I go and prepare a place for you, I will come back and take you to be with me that you also may be where I am" (John 14:2-3).

   "My Father, who has given them to me, is greater than all; no one can snatch them out of my Father's hand" (John 10:29).

Session 6: Your Certificate, Please?

"But God demonstrates His own love for us in this:
While we were still sinners, Christ died for us"
Romans 5:8

Introduction

Faithful is like Stephen, a model martyr who testified boldly, remained true to his convictions, and compassionately prayed for his executioners. Faithful's powerful witness gives courage to some who later begin their own journey to the Celestial City.

Just before it is Christian's turn to burn, he escapes with a new companion, Hopeful, who proves to be another exceptionally valuable friend. Almost immediately, however, they are attracted to what looks like a more pleasant route. Vain Confidence assures them it will take them to the Celestial City. It does not.

Imprisoned in the dungeon of the Giant, Despair, they are almost certain to die—either from starvation or Despair's beatings, or his threat to tear them to pieces. When he provides the means for them to escape through suicide, Christian is seriously tempted. Hopeful reminds him that God is bigger than any giant, and Christian agrees.

Later, Christian is again in the pit of despair when Hopeful reminds him of past victories. Still later, Christian is haunted by visions of their bodies being torn to pieces, and Hopeful suggests they pray. As Christian prays, he coughs, touches his chest, and feels the Key of Promise he was given at the cross. Using the key, they finally escape.

After some time with the Shepherds, during which they learn about the importance of the resurrection, the path of understanding, and the hell of hypocrisy, they are actually able to catch a glimpse of their destination. Ahead lies the last, and perhaps most treacherous, leg of their danger-filled journey.

Session 6: Video Notes

1. Christian and Hopeful, inspired by their glimpse of the Celestial City, receive a map and some final warnings from the Shepherds, and resume their journey. "Beware of the Flatterers," the Shepherd says, "They'll say anything to lead you off the path."

   *"For in his own eyes he **flatters** himself too much to detect or hate his sin"* (Psalm 23:4).

   *"For such people are not serving our Lord Christ, but their own appetites. By smooth talk and **flattery** they deceive the minds of naive people"* (Romans 16:18).

2. Entering the land of Conceit, they meet a young man named Ignorance, who was confident in his own goodness: "No, I didn't come through the gate, and I don't have the scroll, but I'll be fine. I've lived a good life, I've prayed. I've tithed. I've given money to the poor. I've even sacrificed everything in the country just to go to the Celestial City. Yeah, they'll let me in."

   "Jesus answered, 'I am the way and the truth and the life. No one comes to the Father except through me'" (John 14:6).

   Think about it: The old saying "Ignorance is bliss" does not mean that ignorance is right. When ignorance is mistaken—and it almost always is—its bliss turns into agony and regret. Are you, like Ignorance, relying on your own imagination? Beware the land of Conceit.

3. At a fork in the path, Christian and Hopeful think they should go left, but are not sure. An apparent angel convinces them to go right instead.

   "But even if we or an ***angel*** *from heaven should preach a gospel other than the one we preached to you, let him be eternally condemned"* (Galatians 1:8)!

4. The apparent angel praises them for their strength, wisdom, and faith for making it so far along the journey. Soon, however, they sense that they are going in the wrong direction. But before they can escape, they find themselves in the net of the flatterer.

   "Whoever ***flatters*** *his neighbor is spreading a* ***net*** *for his feet"* (Proverbs 29:5).

   Think about it: A network of flattering friends can make each other feel better about bad choices – for a while. Do you have truth-telling friends? What kind of friend are you?

5. HOPEFUL: "If only we would have looked at the map. I bet the answer was there all along."

   "When my spirit grows faint within me, it is you who know my way. In the path where I walk men have hidden a snare for me" (Psalm 142:3).

   "In all your ways acknowledge him, and he will make your paths straight" (Proverbs 3:6).

6. Unable to escape from the net, it appears that the end is near when a true angel shows up.

   "Are not all ***angels*** *ministering spirits sent to serve those who will inherit salvation"* (Hebrews 1:14)?

7. Soon, they meet a well-dressed man coming toward them—away from the direction of the City. He laughs at their destination and says, "After searching for it for many years, I've come to the realization there is no City and there is no God."

   "The fool says in his heart, 'There is no God'" (Psalm 14:1).

8. HOPEFUL (After Being Shaken From His Drowsiness On The Enchanted Ground): "I was like everyone else in Vanity Fair, enjoying all its delights. But I knew that it would have ultimately destroyed me."

"There is a way that seems right to a man, but in the end it leads to death" (Matthew 16:19).

*"He who does what is sinful is of the devil, because the devil has been sinning from the beginning. The reason the Son of God appeared was to **destroy** the devil's work"* (1 John 3:8).

9. HOPEFUL: "God just kept sending me signs, a man of God on the street, a friend that died. I knew that if I died, I would face sudden judgment."

*"Man is destined to die once, and after that to face **judgment**"* (Hebrews 9:27).

10. HOPEFUL: "I became religious. I prayed, I read the Bible…but I really didn't find salvation until I read in the Bible that you can't get right with God through good works."

"He saved us, not because of righteous things we had done, but because of His mercy" (Titus 3:5).

11. THE WORD SPEAKS TO HOPEFUL'S NEED: "Believe in the Lord Jesus Christ, and you shall be saved."

    HOPEFUL: "Lord, how can you forgive a sinner like me?"

    THE WORD (JESUS): "My grace is sufficient. He who comes to me will never be cast out. I will never, ever reject him. I came to the world to save sinners. I am the end of the law of righteousness to everyone that believes. I died for the sins of the world and rose again for the justification of all. I love all. I washed away the sins of the world with my own blood. I am the mediator between God and man."

    HOPEFUL: "That's when I fell in love with Jesus."

12. HOPEFUL: "Is the river deep?"

    ANGEL: "That all depends on how much you trust the King of this place."

    "Then Peter got down out of the boat, walked on the water and came toward Jesus. But when he saw the wind, he was afraid and, beginning to sink, cried out, 'Lord, save me!'

    Immediately Jesus reached out His hand and caught him. 'You of little faith,' He said, 'why did you doubt' " (Matthew 14:30-31)?

    "I tell you the truth, if you have faith as small as a mustard seed, you can say to this mountain, 'Move from here to there' and it will move. Nothing will be impossible for you" (Matthew 17:20).

    "Everything is possible for him who believes" (Mark 9:23).

13. The river became deep, and the waters, rough. It was the evil one's last attempt to stop them. Their thoughts turned to past sins.

    CHRISTIAN: "I'm not going to make it!"

    "The waves of death swirled about me; the torrents of destruction overwhelmed me…In my distress I called to the LORD; I called out to my God…From His temple He heard my voice; my cry came to His ears He reached down from on high and took hold of me; He drew me out of deep waters. He rescued me from my powerful enemy, from my foes, who were too strong for me" (2 Samuel 22:5, 7, 17-18).

14. CHRISTIAN: "My sins are pulling me under."

    HOPEFUL: "Just remember that Jesus cleansed you of your sin."

    "I will forgive their wickedness and will remember their ***sins*** *no more"* (Jeremiah 31:34).

    "As far as the east is from the west, so far has he removed our transgressions from us" (Psalm 103:12).

15. Christian's mind became clouded with doubt, and he could not remember a single promise that the Lord had given him. But Hopeful remembered that Jesus made all things whole. His sins were washed away. He was a new creation.

    "Though your ***sins*** *are like scarlet, they shall be as white as snow; though they are red as crimson, they shall be like wool"* (Isaiah 1:18).

    "Therefore, if anyone is in Christ, he is a new ***creation****; the old has gone, the new has come"* (2 Corinthians 5:17)!

Before continuing to the Discussion Questions, be certain that everyone in the group understands the main message. Our eternal destiny depends on our faith in Jesus Christ to forgive and justify us.

How to Know God

God's greatest expression of love was given to us when He sacrificed His own Son. He did this so that we could know Him personally. Four basic truths explain how this is possible.

1. God loves us and wants us to experience a meaningful life.

   "God so loved the world that He gave His one and only Son, that whoever believes in Him shall not perish but have eternal life" (John 3:16).

2. We are separated from God. God is holy, which means He is perfect. Unfortunately, every person has sinned;

   "All have sinned and fall short of the glory of God" (Romans 3:23).

   Our sin has created a gap that separates us from God; *"the wages of sin is death" (Romans 6:23).* People often try to bridge this gap through their own efforts, but no effort is good enough to meet God's standard of perfection.

   This diagram illustrates our separation from God.

3. God's only provision to bridge this gap is Jesus Christ.

   "But God demonstrates His own love for us in this: While we were still sinners, Christ died for us" (Romans 5:8). Jesus Christ died on the cross to pay the penalty for our sin. He bridged the gap between God and us. *"Jesus answered, 'I am the way and the truth and the life. No one comes to the Father except through me'"* (John 14:6).

   This bridge is a gift from God. *"For it is by grace you have been saved, through faith—and this is not from yourselves, it is the gift of God—not by works, so that no one can boast"* (Ephesians 2:8-9).

   This diagram illustrates how Jesus Christ bridged the gap.

4. Each of us must receive Jesus Christ.

   "To all who received Him, to those who believed in His name, He gave the right to become children of God" (John 1:12).

   Nothing in life compares with knowing Christ personally. We can experience true peace, joy, and hope, when we receive Him as Savior and Lord.

   The choice is yours. You can choose to know God, or you can choose to reject Him.

   If you desire to know the Lord and are not certain whether you have this relationship, you may receive Christ right now. Pray a prayer similar to this one: "Father God, I need you. I invite Jesus to come into my life as my Savior and Lord and make me the person you want me to be. Thank you for forgiving my sins and giving me the gift of eternal life."

   "Believe in the name of the Son of God so that you may know that you have eternal life" (1 John 5:13).

   If you have asked Jesus Christ to come into your life as your Savior, you now know Him and have eternal life. You will live forever with your loving Father God. If you ask Christ into your life, please tell your pastor or someone who will be able to assist you in your spiritual growth.

Session 6: Discussion Questions

Consider the supplied Scriptures as you formulate answers.

1. What would you like to discuss from this video segment?

2. Ignorance is convinced that the scroll [certificate] is unnecessary for entrance into the Celestial city. He's sure his other qualifications will be sufficient. How does it strike you when he is denied entrance and cast into hell simply because he doesn't have the certificate?

   What does the certificate represent?

   [Given at the cross, it represents forgiveness through faith in the sacrifice and resurrection of Jesus. This is the entire basis of our ability to enter heaven. Ignorance was counting on his good works to gain entrance. Although good works are important as a proper and natural response to our new life in Christ, good works can never qualify us for heaven—we can never be good enough; we can never achieve perfection. If we could, there would have been no need for Jesus to die in our place and justify us by grace through faith.]

   "If righteousness could be gained through the law, Christ died for nothing" (Galatians 2:21)!

3. Recall Hopeful's comment after they took the wrong fork in the road: "If only we would have looked at the map. I bet the answer was there all along." When God has given us such a valuable roadmap in the Bible, why are we so reluctant to rely on it?

What will it take for us to develop the right habits for getting God's direction?

"In all your ways acknowledge him, and he will make your paths straight" (Proverbs 3:6).

What does the verse mean when it says, "In all your ways acknowledge him"?

- [Remember that He is above all, aware of all, and in ultimate control of all.
- Maintain an attitude that predetermines obedience (If I know what He wants, I WILL do it).
- Study His Word to know His will.
- Remember that His ways are always higher and better than our ways.
- Pray for direction with an attitude of submission.]

4. Discuss #8 in the Video Notes.

- Have you experienced anything that you later realized could destroy you if you continued in it?

- What has it taught you about God's grace and patience in sparing you?

- Does Satan ever tempt you to presume on God's grace and patience in the future?

"Shall we sin because we are not under law but under grace? By no means! Don't you know that when you offer yourselves to someone to obey him as slaves, you are slaves to the one whom you obey—whether you are slaves to sin, which leads to death, or to obedience, which leads to righteousness" (Romans 6:15-16)?

5. CHRISTIAN: "Please, can you show my wife and children the way?"

   ANGEL: "The King has heard your prayers. He has sent your wife and children an invitation."

   Discuss the importance of intercessory prayer—prayers on behalf of others—as part of our privilege in helping:

   - People we love
   - People who have offended us
   - People who are needy

   "The four living creatures and the twenty-four elders fell down before the Lamb. Each one had a harp and they were holding golden bowls full of incense, which are the prayers of the saints" (Revelation 5:8).

   "The smoke of the incense, together with the prayers of the saints, went up before God from the angel's hand" (Revelation 8:4).

   "I urge, then, first of all, that requests, prayers, intercession and thanksgiving be made for everyone" (1 Timothy 2:1).

APPLICATION

What will you start doing, stop doing, or do differently this week in light of what you have seen or heard in this session?

SCRIPTURE TO MEMORIZE

"He saved us, not because of righteous things we had done, but because of His mercy."
Titus 3:5

Dig Deeper and Learn More

Each session contains optional exercises you may do on your own that will help you learn and apply truths from The Pilgrim's Progress. They include a Scripture to memorize and some questions to answer.

1. "The river became deep, and the waters, rough. It was the evil one's last attempt to stop them. Their thoughts turned to past sins." Notice again how Satan, the accuser, plays both ends against the middle. First he tempts. Then, when he is successful and we give in to sin, he turns around and accuses us—shaming us for our unworthiness.

   What in your past does Satan continue to throw in your face?

   What scriptural promises will you claim to defeat his accusations?

   How will you transform your trust so that it is fully in the righteousness of Christ rather than in your own performance?

Other Notes

Other Notes

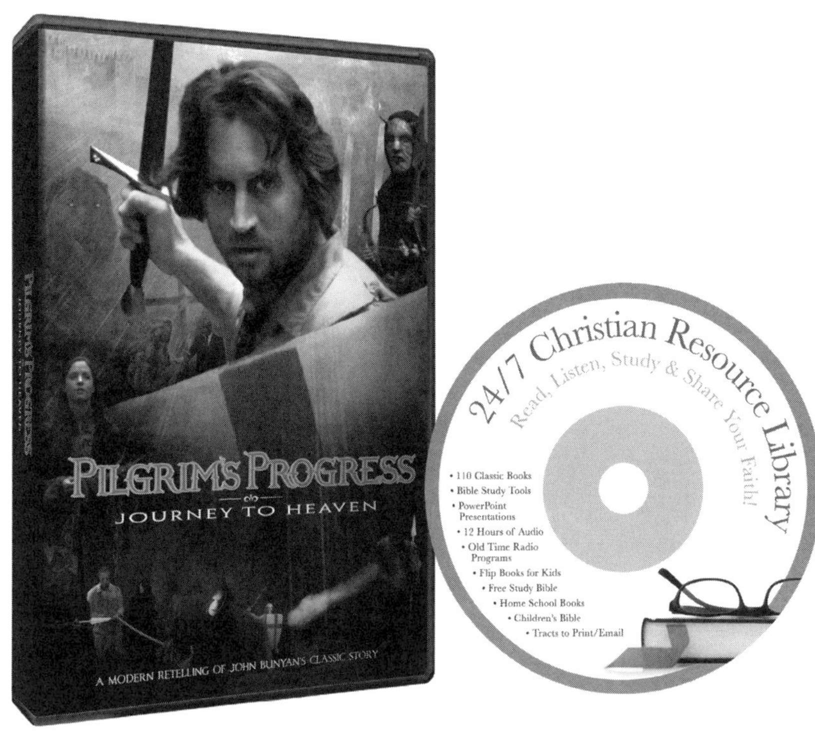

PILGRIM'S PROGRESS: JOURNEY TO HEAVEN is a modern adaptation of John Bunyan's beloved classic. It is the #1 Christian fantasy of all time! The novel has been heralded as a literary masterpiece around the world, as it has been published in over 100 languages and is the most read book other than the Bible.

Amazing visual effects, beautiful locations and a wonderful cast bring to life the story that has inspired each generation for hundreds of years. Follow Christian and his companions on a great Journey from the City of Destruction to the gates of Heaven as they face obstacles large and small, man-made and demon-spawned.

Beyond the gripping drama, Bunyan's powerful allegory teaches us all the hazards and hopes of the Christian life, and it features the triumphant glory that awaits all who faithfully follow the King of kings!

Order Now at www.ReelChristian.com!

FINAL EXIT is considered one of the most effective evangelistic films of the decade as it has helped over 10,000 people dedicate their lives to Christ after viewing this hard-hitting drama. The story revolves around four individuals that are being escorted to judgment by two angels. Who will go to heaven? Who will go to hell? This movie asks the question: If you were to die today, would you go to heaven? It's a great movie to share with lost family members and friends.

THE GATHERING is a powerful portrayal of Christ's return and the coming tribulation. In this film, Michael Carrie, a successful marketing executive is having visions that convinces him the "Second Coming" could happen at any time and does his best to warn his family and friends. Your church and community will enjoy this action filled drama with spectacular special effects

Escape From Hell is about young Dr. Eric Robinson, who becomes obsessed with the idea of an afterlife that leads all people to heaven. Through a series of events that leads to his own death, he finds out that hell is a very real place for those who have rejected the grace and love of Jesus Christ. Don't miss this action packed movie that uses state-of-the-art special effects to take us to Heaven and Hell.

Order Now at www.ReelChristian.com!